INTRODUCTION

Making money on social media involves posting viral content constantly so you can make money from the social media company directly, and also from selling products, posting affiliate links and brand partnerships. The social media companies that pay the most money are Facebook (Meta), Instagram, Threads, Tiktok and X (formerly known as Twitter). With these companies you can get a check every month just for being part of a bonus program and making viral posts that get a lot of attention. You will always get this check as long as you meet their earnings requirements and maintain them.

I will focus on three main social media sites- Facebook (Meta), Tiktok and X. This is because if you figure out Facebook, you can easily figure out the requirements for Instagram and Threads since they are all owned by Meta.

META (FACEBOOK)

First things first, you have to get monetized on Meta if you have not already. To get monetized on Meta, you can check your eligibility in Meta Business Suite (formerly Creator Studio). Download this app if you don't already have it. You can also get a professional dashboard when you change your account to a professional/business account on Meta. Do this first so you can have access to the professional dashboard. You also have to meet the following requirements:

- Page or profile: Have a Meta page or profile in business/professional mode that's at least 30 days old and you're the administrator.
- Followers: Have at least 10,000 followers or more than 250 return viewers.
- Engagement: Have either 50,000 post engagements or 180,000 minutes watched in the last 60 days.
- Country: Be in an eligible country, such as the US, UK, Germany, or India.
- Compliance: Comply with Meta's community standards, payment terms, and page terms.

How to build your followers: There are many ways to

build your followers on Facebook, but I will talk about 3 main ways to do this quickly.

1. **The best way to build your followers on Meta is to follow a whole lot of accounts**. Follow at least 100 accounts a day (or whatever max Meta allows you to follow daily). When you follow at least 100 accounts, 50% of these accounts will follow you back, and that is how you build your followership quickly. When groups/people see you followed them, they are more likely to check out your page and follow you back. When you have reached an acceptable number of followers, you can start unfollowing people/groups who don't follow you back.
2. **Post viral/controversial content**. When you post viral content, more eyes are on your Meta page and most of those that visit end up following you if they like your content. Meta is one of the best platforms to go viral on, just be mindful of copyright infringements and copying other people's work. For photos, make sure you come up with your original caption. You can share or repost photos from other people's posts, but make your own caption. Meta is very restrictive with videos, a lot of viral videos have already been licensed out to big accounts like Unilad and ViralHog, so if you post those videos, they will be flagged and the big accounts will collect revenue from them instead of you. The best way to make viral videos is to make your own viral content or get the video from Tiktok or other social media platforms so that Meta's algorithm won't flag them as copyright content. Moreover, to get viral content for your Meta page, you need to have an Instagram, Youtube, Tiktok, Twitter (X) and Reddit account. The reason you get these accounts on these different platforms is so that you can have access to viral content. Once you open these accounts on Instagram, X, Tiktok, and Reddit, find the

most popular or viral accounts on these platforms and follow them. Next, make sure you have a screen recorder app on your phone, so that as you see these viral videos/pics on the other platforms, you can capture/grab it so you can post it on your Meta account. Every day, you have to go looking for viral content on Instagram, Twitter, Reddit and TikTok. Tiktok and Reddit make it easy to download viral content, but with Instagram and Youtube you might have to screen record with your phone to get the video. Then add your Meta name/tag or website to the video (Using IG or Tiktok editor), add your facial reaction via overlays or voice overs to it to make it your content, and post it on your Meta page with a good caption. Captions that ask obvious questions usually get the most engagement as people respond to the question. As the video goes viral and people watch the video, they'll see your meta tag and possibly follow you and also engage with the post. Another way to get viral content is to make your own. Record yourself doing skits, dancing or giving your opinions on things happening around you. Videos like this do really well on social media and you will build a following in no time. Candid videos of you and your friends/family doing embarrassing or funny things do well on social media also. When you are monetized on Meta, all the interactions on your posts, and the visits to your Meta page will increase your earnings on Meta. Meta pays out every month and you will have to add a bank account to your profile to get the payout.

3. **Follow viral accounts on Meta and continually engage with their content**. Follow viral accounts on Meta like Unilad, ViralHog and TMZ and continually engage with their content. These pages have millions of followers/subscribers so their posts always get a lot of engagement and traffic. Make insightful and surprising comments below their viral posts, and as your comments go viral

under their viral posts, more people will visit your page and possibly follow you. You have to be careful to not say hurtful or offensive comments though, so you don't get reported by people and get your account suspended. Make sure your comments are surprising, but in good taste. Very funny comments also get a lot of engagement. Whatever you do, just make sure your comments/posts are not offensive because Facebook will suspend you sometimes without notice. Avoid using sensitive words on Facebook- words like 'shoot', 'kill', 'abuse' and others will trigger the algorithm of Facebook to focus on your post to see if it is offensive and sometimes, they will take your posts down if they find it offensive. Be very mindful about what you do on Facebook because Facebook is very big on sensitivity and not being offensive to everyone.

How to make more money on Meta: Your followers are growing, you hit 10,000 followers and now you are monetized, what's next? At this point just posting the viral contents you find on other platforms or the ones you create yourself, and continually engaging with your followers will get you paid every month, no matter how small the check is. To increase your income on Meta, you have to find products to sell or brands to promote. As your followers increase, brands/people will approach you to post their content or shout them out on your page for a fee. Be very competitive with your prices and also be mindful of the things you promote on your page. If you spam your followers you could end up losing them. You can also become an Amazon affiliate and just post Amazon products on your page and as people buy the products from Amazon, you get a commission. If you have a business or service, this is the best place to promote your business since most of your posts keep going viral and you are getting multiple visits to your Meta page. If your business has a website, add that to your Meta bio to increase traffic to your website. Also, if you want to promote your other social media platforms, you can add their tags to the viral videos/pics you post on Meta and get more traffic to those pages.

In a nutshell, these methods will increase your income on Meta:

Sponsored Posts: If you have a significant following and engaged audience on Meta, you can partner with brands for sponsored posts and stories. Companies pay you to promote their products, services, or events to your followers. Ensure that the sponsored content aligns with your audience's interests to maintain authenticity.

Affiliate Marketing: Join affiliate programs of companies whose products or services you genuinely recommend. Share affiliate links on Meta, and earn a commission for every sale or referral generated through your links. Disclose your affiliate partnerships transparently to maintain trust with your audience.

Sell Products or Services: If you have your own products or offer services, you can promote them on Meta. Share links to your online store, e-commerce website, or service offerings. Utilize Meta to announce promotions, discounts, and new product launches to attract customers.

Subscriptions: Meta allows your followers to subscribe to your page. You can offer your subscribers exclusive content in their inbox or free shoutouts to your followers for a monthly subscription. Meta will bill your followers monthly and pay you a percentage of whatever subscription amount you choose. This is a great way to get guaranteed money from Meta every month. Meta also gives you the tools to advertise your subscription amount and benefits to your followers.

Create and Sell Digital Products: Develop digital products such as e-books, online courses, webinars, or exclusive content you create and sell them to your Meta followers. Use platforms like Gumroad or Teachable to create, host, and sell your digital products directly to your audience.

Offer Sponsored Content: Besides posts and stories, you can offer sponsored content in the form of sponsored blog posts, sponsored videos, or sponsored live streams. Collaborate with brands to create valuable content that resonates with your audience while promoting the brand's message. You can reach out to big businesses that you are interested in promoting, impress them with the number of followers you have, and get them to pay you to promote their products. Most times these businesses will approach you instead.

Provide Consulting or Coaching Services: If you possess expertise or knowledge in a particular field or industry, offer consulting services or coaching sessions to your

Meta followers. Share valuable insights, tips, and advice related to your niche to establish yourself as an authority figure, and then promote your consulting services. As your following grows and as they engage with you, they will be more likely to pay for your coaching services.

Crowdfunding or Donations: Utilize platforms like Patreon or Ko-fi to receive financial support from your followers. Offer exclusive perks, content, or access to a community for your patrons or supporters. Alternatively, you can also accept donations via platforms like PayPal, Cash App or Gofundme.

Event Promotion: Organize or promote events such as webinars, workshops, conferences, or meetups and sell tickets through Meta. Use Meta to create buzz, share event details, and engage with potential attendees.

Freelancing Opportunities: Meta can be a valuable platform for networking and finding freelancing opportunities. Follow industry-specific hashtags, participate in Meta group chats, and engage with professionals in your field to discover potential freelance gigs or collaborations.

Brand Partnerships and Ambassadorships: Establish strong relationships with brands in your niche and explore opportunities for brand partnerships or ambassadorships. Represent brands authentically, and collaborate on long-term campaigns or projects that align with your values and interests. This type of monetization will probably pay the most because the payouts are usually guaranteed, long term and huge.

TWITTER (X)

Making money on X (formerly known as Twitter) involves posting viral content constantly so you can make money from X directly, and also from selling products, posting affiliate links and brand partnerships.

First things first, you have to get monetized on X if you have not already. You will need at least 500 followers, an average of 5million views total on all your posts in 3 months and also be verified on X (you can easily pay for verification on X). There are two subscription packages that will get you verified on X, the premium and the premium+. Either package will allow you to get monetized, but you have to get these packages in order to be monetized.

How to build your followers on X: There are many ways to build your followers, but I will talk about 3 main ways to do this quickly.

1. **The best way to build your followers on X is to follow a whole lot of accounts.** Follow at least 100 accounts a day (or whatever max X allows you to follow daily). When you follow at least 100 accounts, 50% of these accounts will follow you back, and that is how you build your followership quickly. Don't worry about having a high following/follower ratio, when you have reached an acceptable number of followers, you can start unfollowing people who don't follow you back. Also try

to follow active accounts that will engage with your content. Therefore, checking out the account before following them is very important. You can also screen the type of accounts you follow so you can control what you see on your TL (timeline). If you don't like pornography or abusive content, avoid accounts that always post those. X is also filled with bots so be very mindful to avoid these accounts. X is filled with people that post pornography and abusive content, so if you don't like consuming this type of content, be mindful of the people you follow.

2. **Post viral/controversial content**. When you post viral content, more eyes are on your X page and most of those that visit end up following you if they like your content. X is one of the best platforms to go viral on, there are minimal restrictions to the type of things you can post as opposed to the other social media platforms. Facebook is very restrictive with licensing/copyright laws, Instagram and tiktok have the same problem. Youtube can be restrictive too, but X is very free and almost anything goes. To get viral content for your X page, you need to have a Facebook, Instagram, Youtube, Tiktok and Reddit account. The reason you get these accounts on these different platforms is so that you can have access to viral content. Once you open these accounts on Instagram, Tiktok, Facebook and Reddit, find the most popular or viral accounts on these platforms and follow them. Next, make sure you have a screen recorder app on your phone, so that as you see these viral videos/pics on the other platforms, you can capture/grab it so you can post it on X. Every day, you have to go looking for viral content on Instagram, Reddit, Facebook and TikTok. Tiktok and Reddit make it easy to download viral content, but with Facebook and Instagram you might have to screen record to get the video. Then post it on your X page with a good caption.

Captions that ask obvious questions usually get the most engagement as people respond to the questions. As the video goes viral and people watch the video, they'll see your X account beside the video and possibly follow your X account for more content. When you are monetized on X, all the interactions on your posts, and the visits to your X page will increase your earnings on X. X pays out every 2 weeks and you will have to open a Stripe account where they will pay the money into. X will guide you through this process.

3. **Follow viral accounts on X and continually engage with their content.** Follow viral accounts on X with over 1million followers and continually engage with their content. These pages have millions of followers/subscribers so their posts always get a lot of engagement and traffic. Make insightful and surprising comments below their viral posts, and as your comments go viral under their viral posts, more people will visit your page and possibly follow you. Also copying the link to some of your viral posts and posting it as a comment on some of these pages' content will increase views on your own content.

How to make more money on X: Your followers are growing, you have 500+ followers and hit 5million views in 3months on all your posts and now you are monetized, what's next? At this point just posting the viral contents you find on other platforms and continually engaging with your followers will get you paid every 2 weeks, no matter how small the check is. To increase your income on X, you have to find products to sell or brands to promote. As your followers increase, brands/people will approach you to post their content or shout them out on your page for a fee. Be very competitive with your prices and also be mindful of the things you promote on your page. If you spam your followers you could end up losing them. You can also become an Amazon affiliate and just post Amazon products on your page and as people buy the products from Amazon, you get a commission. If you have a business or service, this is the best place to promote your business since most of your posts keep going viral and you are getting multiple visits to your X page. If your business has a website, add that to your X bio to increase traffic to your website. Also, if you want to promote your other social media platforms, you can add their tags to the viral videos/pics you post on X and get more traffic to those pages.

In a nutshell, these methods will increase your income on X:

Sponsored Tweets: If you have a significant following and engaged audience on X, you can partner with brands for sponsored tweets. Companies pay you to promote their products, services, or events to your followers. Ensure that the sponsored content aligns with your audience's interests to maintain authenticity.

Affiliate Marketing: Join affiliate programs of companies whose products or services you genuinely recommend. Share affiliate links on X, and earn a commission for every sale or referral generated through your links. Disclose your affiliate partnerships transparently to maintain trust with your audience.

Subscriptions: X allows your followers to subscribe to your page. You can offer your subscribers exclusive content in their DMs or free shoutouts to your followers for a monthly subscription. X will bill your followers monthly and pay you a percentage of whatever subscription amount you choose. This is a great way to get guaranteed money from X every month.

Sell Products or Services: If you have your own products or offer services, you can promote them on X. Share links to your online store, e-commerce website, or service offerings. Utilize X to announce promotions, discounts, and new product launches to attract customers.

Create and Sell Digital Products: Develop digital products such as e-books, online courses, webinars, or exclusive content and sell them to your X followers. Use platforms like Gumroad or Teachable to create, host, and sell your digital products directly to your audience.

Provide Consulting or Coaching Services: If you possess expertise in a particular field or industry, offer consulting services or coaching sessions to your X followers. Share valuable insights, tips, and advice related to your niche to establish yourself as an authority figure, and then promote your consulting services.

Crowdfunding or Donations: Utilize platforms like Patreon or Ko-fi to receive financial support from your followers. Offer exclusive perks, content, or access to a community for your patrons or supporters.

Alternatively, you can also accept donations via platforms like PayPal or Cash App.

Event Promotion: Organize or promote events such as webinars, workshops, conferences, or meetups and sell tickets through X. Use X to create buzz, share event details, and engage with potential attendees.

Freelancing Opportunities: X can be a valuable platform for networking and finding freelancing opportunities. Follow industry-specific hashtags, participate in X chats, and engage with professionals in your field to discover potential freelance gigs or collaborations.

Brand Partnerships and Ambassadorships: Establish strong relationships with brands in your niche and explore opportunities for brand partnerships or ambassadorships. Represent brands authentically, and collaborate on long-term campaigns or projects that align with your values and interests.

TIKTOK

Tiktok is one of the most important social media apps today. The app grew so quickly and now other social media platforms are copying some of the features that are featured in Tiktok. Tiktok is currently having some legal trouble with the United States government, but I will cover how to monetize on Tiktok for people outside the United States and also just in case their legal problems with the US government goes away.

Tiktok is not an easy app to make money on. There are a lot of restrictions and policies you have to follow, but once you figure it out, it gets easier to make good, clean money on the app. Tiktok has a program you join that pays you for viral content just like Facebook and Twitter. The name of the program is constantly changing, but I will list the general requirements since that rarely changes. Here are the requirements:

- Page or profile: You can have a personal or business page to monetize on Tiktok. It doesn't matter what type of page you have, but there are more restrictions on business pages than personal pages. For instance, your song selection in a business page is limited and not as exciting as the personal page song selection, so keep that in mind when choosing between a personal page and business page. I would suggest a personal account on Tiktok unless you are running a business and will only be posting exclusive business content.

- Followers: Have at least 10,000 followers and more than 100,000 views in the last 30 days. Earnings will also be based on views and other engagement metrics.
- Country: Be in an eligible country, such as the US, UK, Germany, or India.
- Compliance: Comply with Tiktok's community standards, payment terms, and page terms. Tiktok, just like Meta, is sensitive to offensive and abusive content. Be very mindful of this when you make posts and use sensitive/offensive words on Tiktok. Your posts also have to be a minute long or more to generate money, so keep that in mind when you are monetized and seeking to post content to make money.

How to build your followers on Tiktok: There are many ways to build your followers on Tiktok, but I will talk about 3 main ways to do this quickly.

1. **The best way to build your followers on Tiktok is to follow a whole lot of accounts**. Follow at least 100 accounts a day (or whatever max Tiktok allows you to follow daily). When you follow at least 100 accounts, 50% of the accounts will follow you back, and that is how you build your followership quickly. Don't worry about having a high following/follower ratio, when you have reached an acceptable number of followers, you can start unfollowing people who don't follow you back. You can also follow people who engage with your content, that is a guaranteed way to know if a page is active and you can check their follower/following ratio to see how

likely they are to follow you back. If they follow more pages than are following them back, they are more likely to follow you back. If they have a lot of followers but are following back a small percentage of people, they more than likely will not follow you, don't even waste your time with people like this.

2. **Post viral/controversial content and go live often.** When you post viral content, more eyes are on your Tiktok page and most of those that visit end up following you if they like your content. To get viral content for your Tiktok page, you need to have a Facebook, Instagram, Youtube and Reddit account. The reason you get these accounts on these different platforms is so that you can have access to viral content. Once you open these accounts on Instagram, Facebook and Reddit, find the most popular or viral accounts on these platforms and follow them. Next, make sure you have a screen recorder app on your phone, so that as you see these viral videos/pics on the other platforms, you can capture/grab it so you can post it on Tiktok. Tiktok loves engagement and voice over videos, so personal videos about experiences or reviews do really well on Tiktok. Don't worry too much about the One minute or more video requirement at the beginning, just worry about getting your followership to 10,000 followers. When you are monetized on Tiktok, then you can worry about the length of your videos and the content of your videos to ensure you are getting paid for your work. Tiktok also loves content creators who have engaging live sessions on their platform. Going live and keeping people engaged will give you access to a lot of visibility and people can follow you from your live sessions.

3. **Follow viral people on Tiktok and continually engage with their content.** Follow viral accounts on Tiktok and continually engage with their content. These pages have millions of followers/subscribers so their posts always

get a lot of engagement and traffic. Make insightful and surprising comments below their viral posts, and as your comments go viral under their viral posts, more people will visit your page and possibly follow you.

How to make more money on Tiktok: Your followers are growing, you hit 10,000 followers and more than 100,000 views in the last 30 days and now you are monetized, what's next? At this point just posting viral content will you get you paid on Tiktok, no matter how small the check is. To increase your income on Tiktok, you have to find products to sell or brands to promote. As your followers increase, brands/people will approach you to post their content or shout them out on your page for a fee. Be very competitive with your prices and also be mindful of the things you promote on your page. If you spam your followers you could end up losing them. You can also become a Tiktok shop affiliate and just promote Tiktok shop products on your page and as people buy the products from Tiktok shop, you get a commission. If you have a business or service, this is the best place to promote your business since most of your posts keep going viral and you are getting multiple visits to your Tiktok page. If your business has a website, add that to your Tiktok bio to increase traffic to your website. Also, if you want to promote your other social media platforms, you can add their tags to the viral videos/pics you post on Tiktok and get more traffic to those pages.

In a nutshell, these methods will increase your income on Tiktok:
Sponsored Content: If you have a significant following and engaged audience on Tiktok, you can partner with

brands for sponsored content. Companies pay you to promote their products, services, or events to your followers. Ensure that the sponsored content aligns with your audience's interests to maintain authenticity.

Subscriptions: Tiktok allows your followers to subscribe to your page. You can offer your subscribers exclusive content in live sessions and interact with them personally during your live sessions. Tiktok will bill your followers monthly and pay you a percentage of whatever subscription amount you choose. This is a great way to get guaranteed money from Tiktok every month.

Sell Products or Services: Tiktok shop is always inviting content creators to join their affiliate program. Once you are invited, you will have access to the Tiktok Seller center and can sell Tiktok products directly on the app. You can get Tiktok shop merchandise by buying them, or sometimes vendors can send you these products to test for free, depending on how viral and engaging you are. Once you use these products and make a video reviewing them, you can post these videos with a link to the product on your page. When people buy the product through your link, you will get a percentage of the sale. People have made millions doing this.

Brand Partnerships and Ambassadorships: Establish strong relationships with brands and Businesses in your niche and explore opportunities for brand partnerships or ambassadorships. Represent brands authentically, and collaborate on long-term campaigns or projects that align with your values and interests. They can pay you directly for promotional content and shoutouts that you can post to your Tiktok page and your followers.

Tips and Donations: Tiktok has a tipping feature that allows some creators to earn money from tips and donations. Fans of your content can use this to show gratitude and support for your content. Your fans can send you virtual gifts and coins. Most of these gifts can be collected during live streams. In fact, it is important that you go live so you can get these virtual gifts. You can redeem these gifts and coins for Diamonds which is Tiktok's digital currency. You can trade in your Diamonds for real cash.

Regardless of the monetization method and social media apps you choose, focus on providing value to your audience, maintaining authenticity, and building genuine relationships. Continue building your follower numbers on these platforms, the more followers you have, the more money you make. Consistently engage with your followers, share valuable content, and adapt your strategies based on audience feedback and market trends.

BE CAREFUL

As your following on these platforms grow, there will be hackers that will try to hack your account so they can take over your account and have access to your followers. They will send you alarming messages with links and ask you to verify your account and click the links to log back into your account. Some will act like brands that want to partner with you and send you links to click on and sign in for them to pay you.

Never click any links that are sent to you in a message or email. Whenever you get a message that requires you to sign into your social media account, always go back to the app and sign in yourself. Never sign in from any links or emails because it could be a phishing attempt to get your login information so they can sign into your account and take over your account.

Always use 2-step verification for all your social media accounts. This is very important. There should always be an extra step of email or text message if someone tries to sign into your account from a different device or region. I get notifications on my viral social media pages of people trying to sign in from Asia, Europe or Africa all the time. A lot of people have lost social media accounts with millions of followers to hackers, so be very careful. Your viral social media page is literally worth thousands of dollars, so protect it very well.

CONCLUSION

There is a lot of money to be made online. Social media is making a lot of millionaires daily, so don't ignore this new aspect of wealth creation. Gone are the days people who spend hours on social media are considered foolish and lazy, these days they are making more money than people with regular paying jobs.

I hope with these tips, you can find success with monetizing your social media pages and get into a system of wealth creation that is relatively cheap to start (all you need is a good cell phone camera, a good cell phone stand, some good lighting and maybe a friend to help you film when you can't film alone. I wish you success in all your endeavors.

www.ingramcontent.com/pod-product-compliance
Lightning Source LLC
Chambersburg PA
CBHW071002220526
45471CB00007B/3144